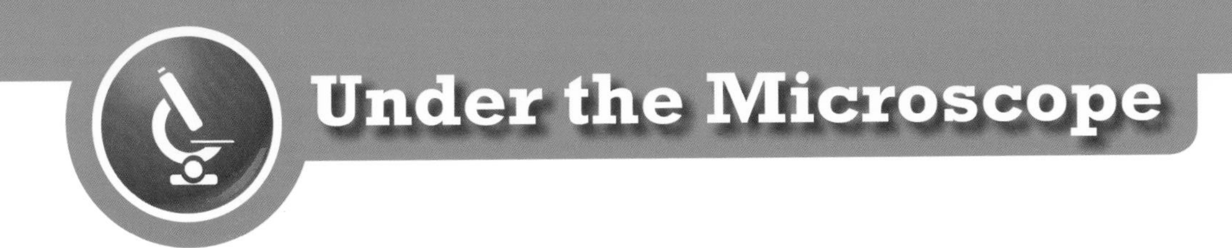

In Your Food

Sabrina Crewe

Consultant:
Professor Anne K. Camper,
Montana State University

Chelsea Clubhouse
An imprint of Chelsea House
132 West 31st Street
New York NY 10001

Library of Congress Cataloging-in-Publication Data
Crewe, Sabrina.
In your food / Sabrina Crewe ; consultant, Anne K. Camper.
p. cm. -- (Under the microscope)
Includes index.
ISBN 978-1-60413-824-5
1. Food--Microbiology--Juvenile literature. I. Title.
QR115.C74 2010
664.001'579--dc22
2009043207

Chelsea Clubhouse books are available at special discounts when purchased in bulk quantities for businesses, associations, institutions, or sales promotions. Please call our Special Sales Department in New York at (212) 967-8800 or (800) 322-8755.

You can find Chelsea Clubhouse on the World Wide Web at http://www.chelseahouse.com

Text design by Sabine Beaupré
Illustrations by Stefan Chabluk
Originated by Discovery Books
Composition by Discovery Books
Cover printed by Bang Printing, Brainerd, MN
Book printed and bound by Bang Printing, Brainerd, MN
Date printed: May 2010
Printed in the United States of America

10 9 8 7 6 5 4 3 2 1

This book is printed on acid-free paper.

All links and Web addresses were checked and verified to be correct at the time of publication. Because of the dynamic nature of the Web, some addresses and links may have changed since publication and may no longer be valid.

Acknowledgments
We would like to thank the following for permission to reproduce photographs: Centers for Disease Control and Prevention, US Department of Health and Human Services: p. 22; Sabrina Crewe: p. 29; Dennis Kunkel Microscopy, Inc.: pp. 6, 19, 20, 23, 26; Science Photo Library: pp. 5 (Clouds Hill Imaging Ltd.), 7 right (David Scharf), 10 (Scimat), 13 (Andrew Syred), 15 (Biophoto Associates), 18 (Scimat); Shutterstock Images: pp. 4 (Jacek Chabraszewskiin), 7 left (Optimarc), 9 (Julián Rovagnatin), 11 (Alexey Chernitevich), 12 (Georgy Markov), 16 (Mayer Kleinostheim), 17 (Carolina K. Smith), 21 (Alena Brozova), 24 (Razumovskaya Marina Nikolaevna), 25 (Nice_pictures); US Department of Agriculture: pp. 14, 27.

Contents

Some words are **bold** the first time they appear in the text. These words are explained in the glossary at the back of this book.

Yogurt is a healthy food partly because of the **microbes** that live in it. We will find out more about these microbes.

What Are You Eating?

You probably think you know what is in the food you are eating. You may be surprised, however, when you see your food under a microscope. Microscopes allow us to see things up close and look at them in a different way. Under the microscope, we can see the tiny parts that foods are made of. We can learn why foods change when we cook them or when they spoil.

Sharing your food

The microscope also shows us that you may not be the only one eating your food! In the refrigerator or on the kitchen counter, tiny **organisms** (living things) may also be munching away.

Microorganisms and microbes

Organisms too small to see are called **microorganisms**. They range from tiny animals that you could find with a magnifying glass to living things so small you could fit thousands of them on a grain of salt.

Microorganisms that are not animals are often called microbes. Some of these make our food rot. Others make us sick if we eat them. Other microbes actually make food healthy or give it a good taste.

Food up close

Let's take a look at your food under the microscope and discover what you are really eating. By looking first at two everyday foods—bread and milk—we're going to learn about two important kinds of microorganisms with which we share our food and our world.

Micro-Monster

The flour **mite** could live in your kitchen cabinet in a package of flour. In real life, this mite is 0.3 to 0.5 of a millimeter long, so you could see it with a magnifying glass. This is what it looks like when it is magnified 200 times.

Bread and Microfungi

Fungi are a type of organism that includes the mushrooms we eat. But there are much tinier fungi that are part of some foods. These microscopic forms of fungi are known as **microfungi**.

Food invaders

First, let's look at some microfungi that are invaders. Fungi spread through their food source with threads called **hyphae**. And their food source may well be your food source!

Fungi feed on living things and organic matter (things that were once alive or come from living things). As they do so, they break down their food by releasing chemicals into it.

These are **spores** of *Mucor*, a microfungus that spreads through bread and makes it moldy.

Moldy bread

Mold is a type of fungus that invades food and breaks it down, causing it to spoil. If you look at a slice of bread and see a patch of mold, you are actually seeing a fungus feeding on the bread. The mold is a network of hyphae called a mycelium.

As the mycelium spreads, the hyphae grow fruiting bodies that hold spores, which are like tiny seeds. When the fruiting bodies release the spores, they travel in the air to find new food to grow on.

How Small Is Small?

An average yeast cell is about 4 **micrometers** across. There are 1,000 micrometers in a millimeter, so you could line up 250 yeast cells alongside just 1 millimeter on your ruler. You could fit more than 6,000 alongside 1 inch.

Making bread

Yeasts are different from regular fungi. They only have one **cell**. Carbohydrates—sugar and **starch**—are the yeast cell's favorite food. When yeast is mixed with flour and water to make bread, the yeast cells begin to feed on the starch in the flour. This process, called **fermentation**, releases carbon dioxide bubbles. The bubbles make the bread swell up, or rise. After the bread is cooked, the bubbles appear as holes.

You can see the holes in this bread made by the yeast releasing gas bubbles.

These yeast cells are budding to reproduce themselves. The bud comes off to make a new yeast cell. These cells have been magnified 4,000 times.

Milk and Bacteria

The smallest and most plentiful microorganisms in our food—and in the world—are **bacteria**. Even though you can't see them without a microscope, bacteria are everywhere.

What are bacteria?

So what are these microscopic life-forms? Unlike plants and animals, bacteria are made of a single cell. You can see a typical bacterium below and take a look inside its cell. Bacteria often live in large clumps called colonies. They multiply constantly by dividing their cells.

Most bacteria are shaped like rods, but many are round. Others are bent or shaped like spirals. Bacteria also vary in size, but most measure between 1 and 4 micrometers across.

Whatever shape bacteria are, the insides of their cells hold the same basic parts. On the outside, some bacteria have pili to hold onto the cells of their food source. The larger hairs are flagella, which many bacteria use to move around.

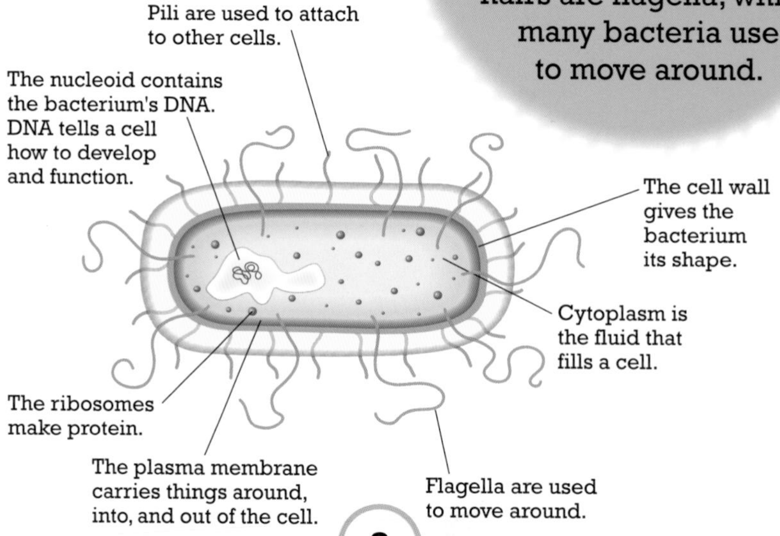

Pili are used to attach to other cells.

The nucleoid contains the bacterium's DNA. DNA tells a cell how to develop and function.

The cell wall gives the bacterium its shape.

Cytoplasm is the fluid that fills a cell.

The ribosomes make protein.

The plasma membrane carries things around, into, and out of the cell.

Flagella are used to move around.

Hungry bacteria

Bacteria need food to survive. Mostly they live on organic matter—food that comes from living things—just like we do. As bacteria digest food, they change the food they are eating.

Living in milk

Milk contains bacteria called *lactobacilli* that live on lactose, the sugar in milk. When milk goes sour, it's because *lactobacilli* are producing a sour substance called lactic acid as they feed.

Nobody wants to drink sour milk, but we can use the bacteria in milk to make food we do like. Next you will see how bacteria and fungi together help make some of our favorite foods!

Bacterial Names

Scientists use the term *bacilli* to describe rod-shaped bacteria and *cocci* for bacteria shaped like spheres. These bacteria shapes are common in milk. *Lacto* means milk, so some milk bacteria are named *lactobacilli* and others are *lactococci*.

Yogurt and Cheese

There are many thousands of bacterial **species**. And those are just the ones scientists know about —there are more being discovered every year. Several kinds of bacteria help to turn milk into foods we eat every day.

This picture shows *Streptococcus thermophilus* (orange beads) and *Lactobacillus bulgaricus* (blue rods) bacteria in yogurt. Both these bacteria can fight bad bacteria that make us sick.

Making yogurt

Two bacteria often used to make yogurt are *Streptococcus thermophilus* and *Lactobacillus bulgaricus*. First the milk is heated to condense it (reduce its liquid content to make it thicker), and then the bacteria are added. With the milk sugars to feed on, the bacteria multiply quickly. They go to work on the milk, thickening it and giving it a yogurty taste.

Good bacteria in food can help us digest food. They also compete with bad bacteria in our bodies.

Ripening cheese

Cheese is made from the protein in milk. First, bacteria produce the acid that separates the protein from the liquid part of the milk. The protein forms soft, solid stuff called curd. Curd makes unripened cheeses, such as cottage cheese.

The curd can then be ripened with the help of other microbes that harden cheese and give it flavor. Different microbes—either bacteria or fungi—produce different kinds of cheese. The bacteria that make Swiss cheese, for example, are called *propionibacteria*. They release gas bubbles, and when the cheese hardens, there are holes where the bubbles were.

Micro-Scientist

Scientists who are bacteria experts are called bacteriologists. They study the effects of bacteria on food, on people's bodies, and on the environment.

Blue cheese

Blue cheese ripens with the help of fungi. We learned earlier how fungi spread through bread. When the mold *Penicillium roqueforti* is put into cheese, it also starts to spread and form blue veins in the cheese.

The veins you see in blue cheese are the hyphae and spores of the fungus *Penicillium roqueforti*.

Fruit

Many forms of life, from bugs down to the tiniest microbes, like fruit as much as we do. Fruit is full of sugar, and many microorganisms use sugar as their food source.

You can see by looking at this moldy apple that fungi like to feed on fruit sugars.

How yeast ferments fruit

We saw earlier how yeast likes to feed on the starch in flour. Yeast cells will also feed on fruit, where you can see them form a powdery surface. When yeast consumes the sugar in fruit, it converts it into two products: carbon dioxide, which is a gas, and ethanol, which is a liquid alcohol. This is a form of fermentation. Ethanol is the alcohol in wine and other alcoholic drinks, so yeast is used to make these drinks. Wine, for example, is made from fermented grapes.

Viruses

The smallest of all known microbes are **viruses**. Viruses are not really organisms. They are chemical clusters that invade the cells of living things and eventually destroy them. Viruses can kill people, and they can also get into fruit crops and destroy them. Fruit viruses are often spread from one plant to another by aphids (tiny pests that feed on the plants).

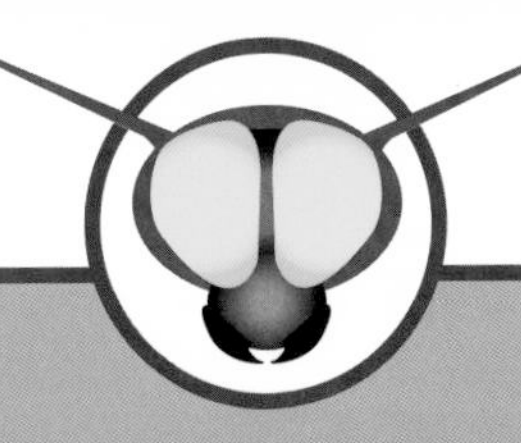

Micro-Monster

When fruit begins to decay, it attracts tiny insects called fruit flies. Fruit flies like to feed on the alcohol produced by fermenting fruit. They do this with the spongy mouthparts you can see at the bottom of this photo between the fly's legs. Female fruit flies will lay their eggs on the fruit. Before you know it, the eggs hatch, the fruit is covered in more fruit flies, and your kitchen can become infested!

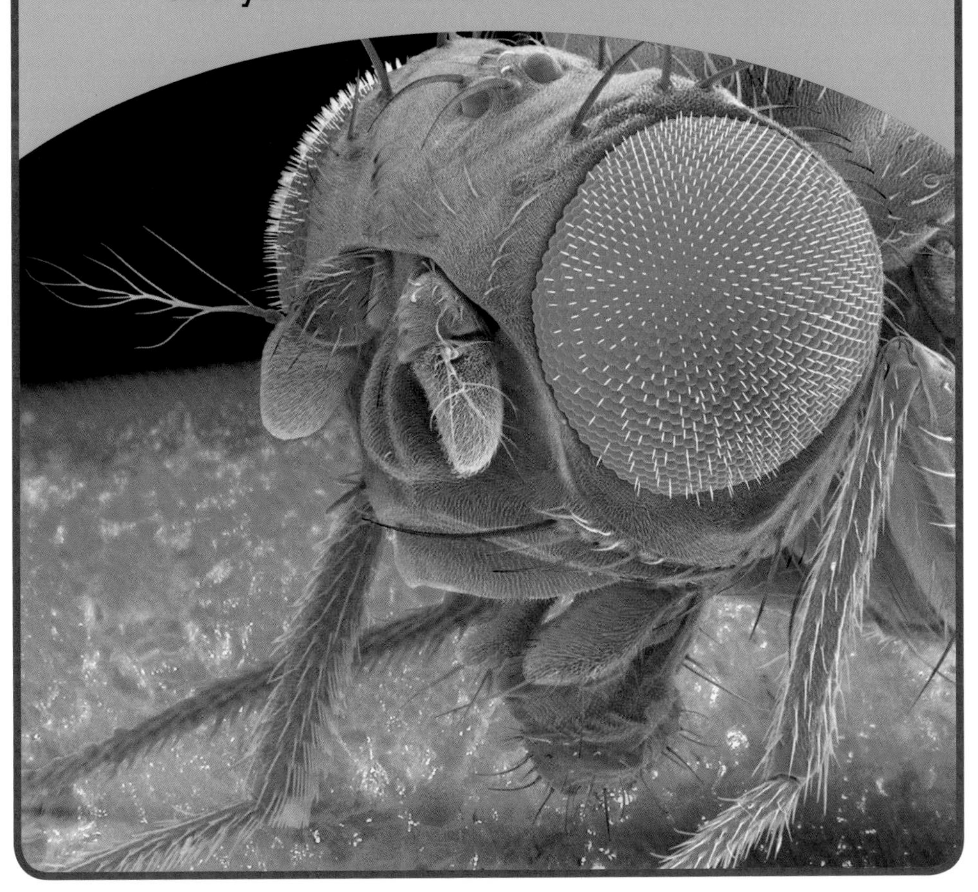

Vegetables and Grains

All kinds of microorganisms live on vegetables and grains. They are found on growing crops and on produce in your home.

Micro-enemies

Unfortunately, there are many insects, bacteria, fungi, and viruses that destroy grain and vegetable crops. Insects too small to see can eat their way through a whole field of vegetables. More than 5,000 types of fungi attack food crops with diseases such as rust, smut, blight, and mildew.

Helping crops grow

Other bacteria, microfungi, and **microanimals** have useful roles to play when crops are growing. These microorganisms keep soil healthy and prey on pests.

The bacterium *Bacillus thuringiensis* protects crops because it makes a substance that harms pests. Farmers and gardeners can spray the bacteria on plants without any harm to people, animals, plants, or the environment.

Phytophthora infestans is a fungus that attacks potatoes and gives them blight. Infected potatoes that seem healthy when they are growing may rot later after you bring them home from the store.

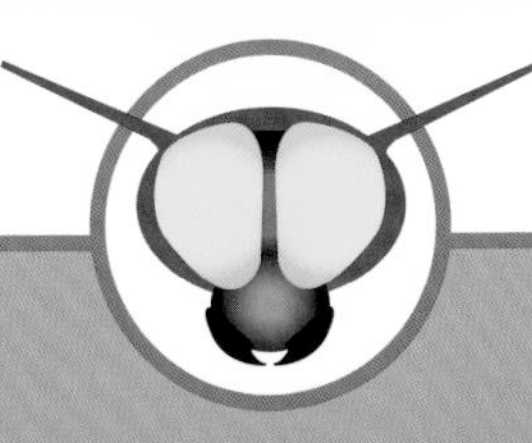

Micro-Monster

The grain weevil, like other weevils, has a long snout, or rostrum, with its mouth at the end. Grain weevils use their rostrums to make holes in kernels of grain stored in granaries or homes. Female grain weevils lay their eggs right in these holes, so their young have a ready-made source of food when they hatch. Because they are so tiny, you would never know the **larvae** were inside the grains in your kitchen. The grain weevils eat and grow inside the kernel until they are ready to come out, as the one in this photo is doing.

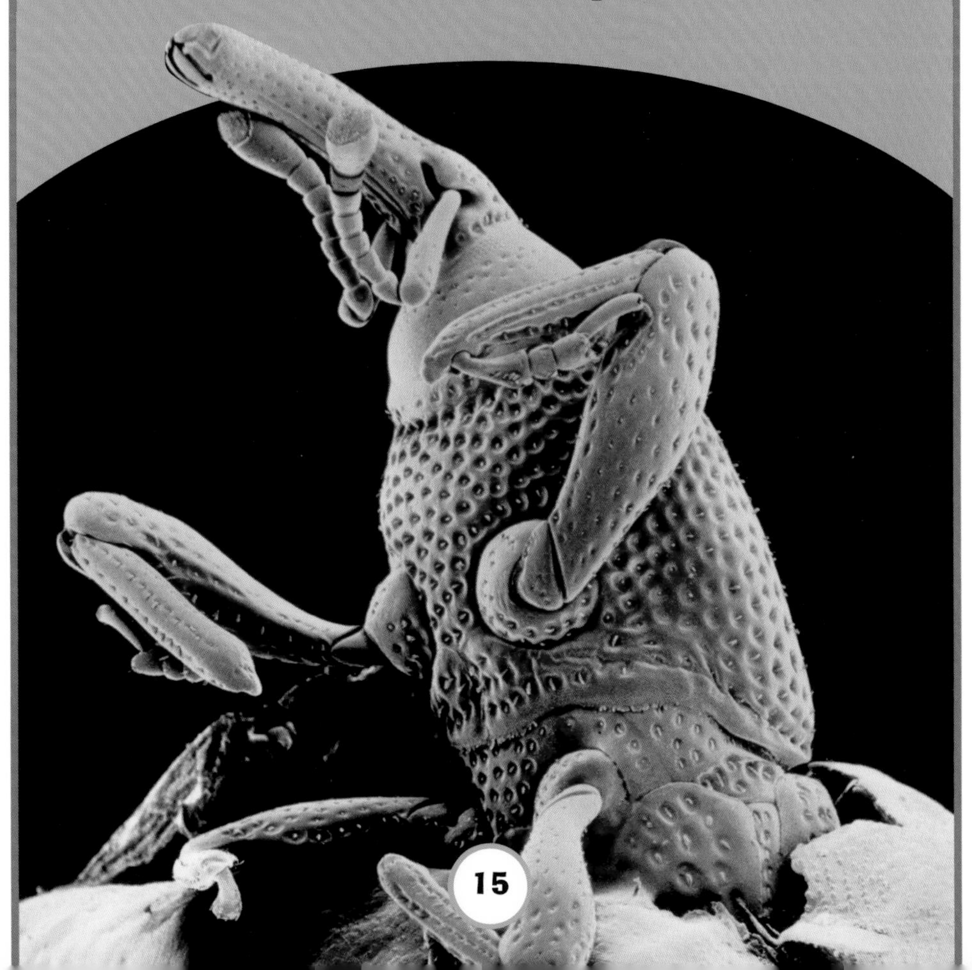

Magnified Meat

There are lots of microorganisms that feed and grow on meat. When you see flies buzzing around your kitchen, you should make sure your meat is covered up!

Maggots

Flies like to lay their eggs on meat, and you probably won't notice them because they are so tiny. When the eggs hatch, the maggots that come out will start eating the meat. They do this by squirting their saliva on the meat to soften it. Then they suck up the meaty liquid.

How Small Is Small?

A pile of 50 fly eggs is about the same size as the tip of your pencil.

Maggots start out tiny, but they are easy to see after they have been feeding and growing for a few days.

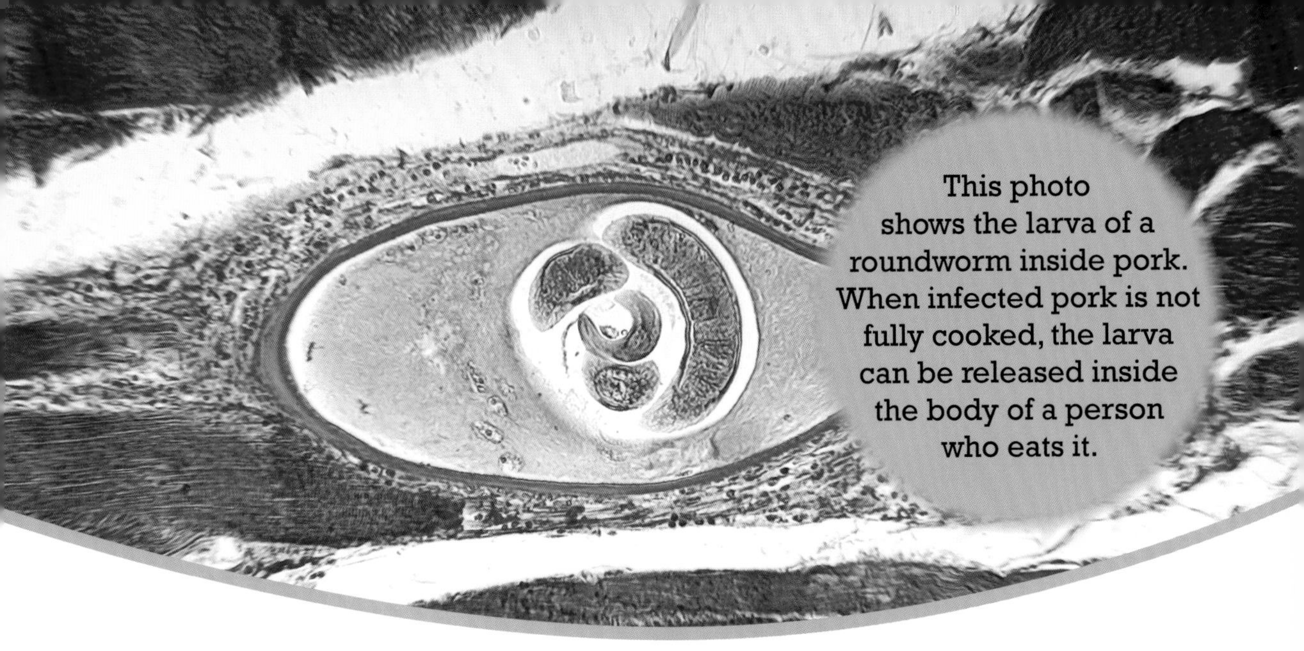

This photo shows the larva of a roundworm inside pork. When infected pork is not fully cooked, the larva can be released inside the body of a person who eats it.

Parasites

Organisms that live on or in other living things are called **parasites**. Some microanimals are parasites that live in people's bodies. The meat we eat may contain microscopic parasite eggs. When you eat meat containing live eggs or larvae, a parasite can hatch, mature, and make its home inside your intestine.

Cooking Chemistry

Have you ever thought about why we cook foods? Cooking heats food and causes it to change. When we cook meat, we are changing its structure. Cooking opens up the microscopic coils of protein **molecules** in meat tissues. As the protein uncoils, the meat becomes tender, tastier, and easier to chew. And if your meat is infected with parasites, the heat from cooking can kill them off. That's another reason to make sure meat is well cooked.

Meat Microbes

As we saw earlier, bacteria absorb their food from other livings things or from decaying matter. Many bacteria can digest protein, so they live on meat. With the right supply of food, bacteria multiply quickly, so a small piece of meat can hold millions of bacteria.

This meat has been infected by both *Salmonella* and *Escherichia coli* bacteria.

Food poisoning

We know that most bacteria are harmless and even useful. But some of these microscopic organisms can also be very harmful. Several bacteria that infect meat can give people food poisoning. Most kinds of food poisoning have the same horrible symptoms. People feel nauseous, and they vomit a lot. They get really bad stomachaches and diarrhea. People usually recover after a few days, but sometimes they develop more serious illnesses.

Bad bacteria

Let's look at some of the bacteria in meat that make us sick. *Salmonella* bacteria can invade all kinds of meat.

They are common in chicken, so eggs can be infected, too. It takes fewer than 20 *Salmonella* cells to make someone sick.

Campylobacter jejuni is even more common than *Salmonella* in chicken. People infected with this bacterium get terrible diarrhea. Usually it goes away by itself, and people may not know what caused the illness.

Good and bad *E. coli*

Some forms of the bacterium *Escherichia coli* (*E. coli* for short) are healthy. They live in our intestines and fight other, harmful bacteria. But one type of *E. coli* that lives in cattle intestines can make people sick. When beef is ground into hamburger, the *E. coli* often infects meat and gets passed on to humans. Other harmful types of *E. coli* come from infected chicken or even vegetables.

Antibiotics

Antibiotics are substances that can kill bacteria in your body. We use them as medicines when we get sick from bacterial infections. In the photo below, an antibiotic is destroying an *E. coli* cell wall. Farmers and ranchers add antibiotics to animal feed to prevent illness in cows, pigs, and sheep. But some bacteria are getting so used to antibiotics that the antibiotics can't kill them anymore. So when bacteria cause infections, antibiotics may not be able to kill the bacteria and make people better.

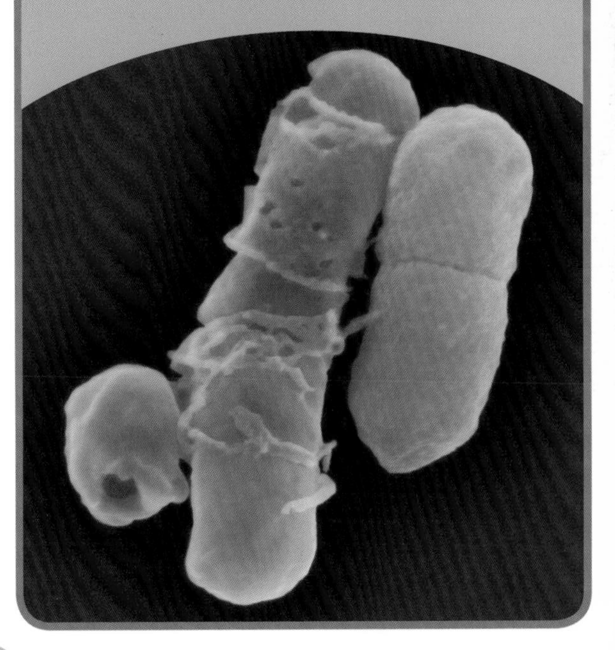

Pantry Pests

As we've seen, many microorganisms like to eat the same stuff as we do. Even when food is stored in a package or a can, bugs and microbes can find ways to get at it.

Pests in the package

Take a look at the packages in your kitchen cabinets or pantry. You'll probably see flour, cereals, rice, pasta, baking mix, crackers, and maybe some nuts and popcorn. Bugs love to get into dried foods like these. If you see tiny beetles, moths, or worms on your counter, you may find they are also in your food.

This weevil was found in a package of rice. It is covered in rice dust.

Packages and containers don't have to be open for bugs to get in. Many bugs can chew through packaging, and arrive in your kitchen already inside the package. Beetles, moths, and mites lay their eggs where there will be a good food source for larvae when they hatch. They often do this while food is stored in warehouses or on its way to the store.

Canned bacteria

Clostridia are bacteria that thrive without oxygen. Cans of food can be infected by *Clostridia* if their contents aren't properly processed. The *Clostridia* produce a gas that makes cans swell up. Some *Clostridia* can also cause botulism, a very serious kind of food poisoning.

Chocolate

Believe it or not, microorganisms help give chocolate its yummy taste. Chocolate is made from cocoa, which comes from the cacao bean. As part of the chocolate-making process, the beans are fermented by bacteria and yeast. When these microorganisms feed on the cacao, they break down its molecules, releasing chemicals that will create a chocolate flavor.

What's in the Water?

We rely on water just as much as we rely on food. And we take it for granted that the water in our homes is pure and safe to drink. Mostly it is, but not always. And there are many places in the world where drinking water can be as **contaminated** as some of the foods we've looked at.

Protists

Many of the microscopic life-forms that find their way into drinking water are **protists**. Protists are usually single-celled microorganisms that live in water or damp places.

You will remember we read about parasites that can get into our bodies from food and live inside us. Some protists can become parasites inside us if we drink the water that contains them.

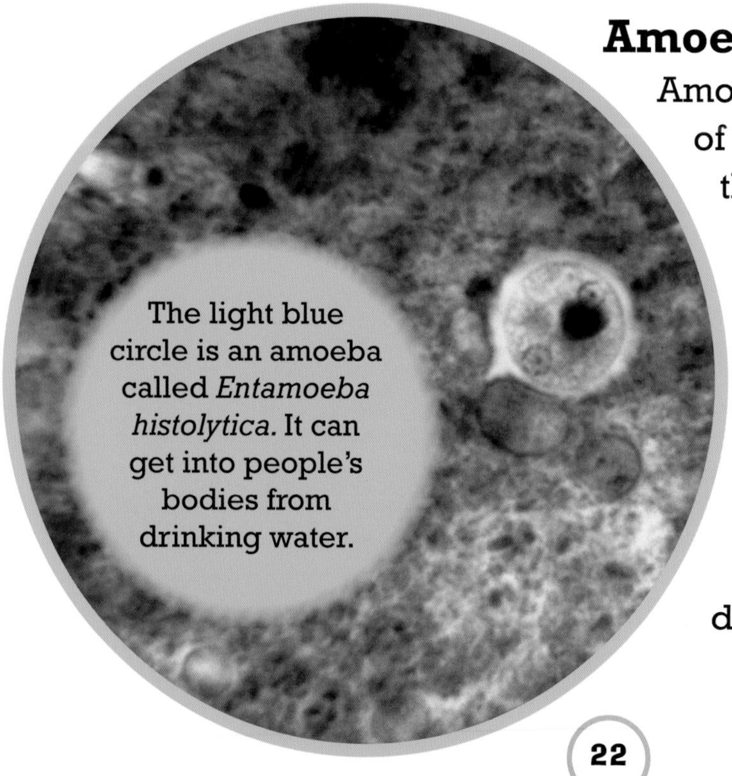

The light blue circle is an amoeba called *Entamoeba histolytica*. It can get into people's bodies from drinking water.

Amoebas

Amoebas are one kind of protist. Even though they consist of just one cell and look like a shapeless blob, amoebas can move around and even catch food to eat!

Like bacteria, amoebas can reproduce just by dividing themselves.

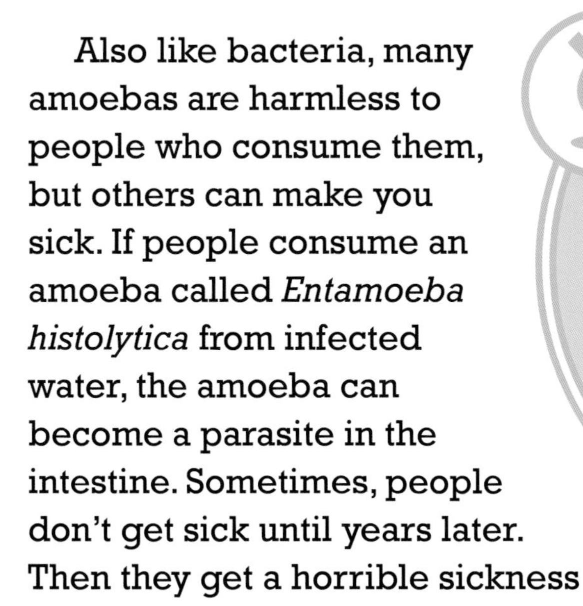

Also like bacteria, many amoebas are harmless to people who consume them, but others can make you sick. If people consume an amoeba called *Entamoeba histolytica* from infected water, the amoeba can become a parasite in the intestine. Sometimes, people don't get sick until years later. Then they get a horrible sickness call dysentery, which gives them painful symptoms like those of food poisoning.

How Small Is Small?

The *Entamoeba histolytica* is 15 to 20 micrometers long. There can be thousands of them in one drop of water.

Giardia

Giardia lamblia is another protist that infects people's intestines. It can exist in water in a dormant (inactive) stage called a **cyst**. When it gets into your body, it becomes an active parasite and can give you a nasty illness called giardiasis. Infections from *Giardia* can last for a long time.

The *Giardia lamblia* protist has several flagella—the whip-like tails it uses to move around.

It's important to keep kitchen cloths clean to avoid spreading bacteria from one food to another.

Keeping Food Safe

After learning all about microscopic life in your food, you might be getting a little concerned. Don't worry—most food is safe and healthy most of the time. And there are things you can do to make sure you keep your food free from microscopic invaders.

Keeping clean

Many kitchen bacteria are helpful or at least harmless. They will compete with harmful bacteria to keep food safe. You can help, too, by keeping things clean, and the most important thing to keep clean is you! Bacteria will travel quickly from your skin onto food. It's really important to wash your hands after petting animals, using the bathroom, and playing outside. Never forget to wash your hands before touching food.

Micro-Fact

Remember that microfungi spread by releasing invisible spores. If you wrap or cover foods in the refrigerator, fungi spores can't travel from one food to another.

You may be surprised to know that the sponges and cloths we use for cleaning hold more bacteria than anything else! Bacteria can spread from a sponge to a dish and then to your food. Sponges and cloths need to be washed in very hot water or even heated in the microwave for two minutes to kill bacteria.

Hot and cold

Bacteria multiply faster in warm conditions. To slow decay, keep meat, produce, and dairy foods in the refrigerator or freezer.

Proper heating and cooking will kill bacteria altogether. For example, *Salmonella* in eggs, chicken, and red meat die when these foods are thoroughly cooked.

Storing Foods

To keep bugs and fungi out of packaged food, make sure it is safely stored away. Put dried food in metal or glass containers because bugs won't chew through these. Don't leave crumbs on the table and counter—insects will be attracted to them, and once they arrive, they will lay eggs and multiply!

Inside Food Cells

When you look at food under the microscope you can see the parts it is made of. Food from living things, such as plants or animals, is made up of cells.

Looking inside a cell

If you magnify food even more, you can see the parts inside cells. Earlier, we looked at DNA inside a bacterial cell. Although DNA is unimaginably tiny, it is important. DNA is a molecule that controls what a cell becomes.

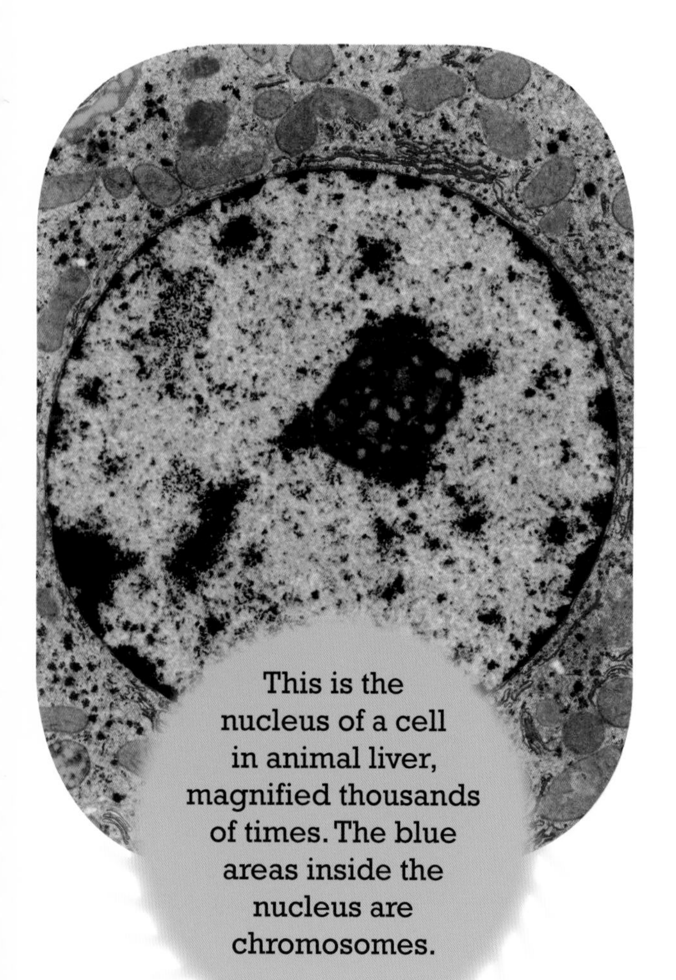

This is the nucleus of a cell in animal liver, magnified thousands of times. The blue areas inside the nucleus are chromosomes.

DNA and genes

Every cell in plants and animals also has DNA inside its **nucleus**. Long strings of DNA are packaged into microscopic units called chromosomes. The DNA in chromosomes forms sets of instructions, called genes, for the cell to follow. Because of genes, tomato cells form a tomato, and chicken cells turn into a chicken. Because of genes, the tomatoes might be bright red or pale orange.

Changing Genes

You may have heard people talk about genetically modified (GM) foods. But what does that mean? Modify means adapt or change, so GM foods are foods that have had their genes changed. Scientists change genes by taking DNA from one type of plant, for example, and putting them into another. Why would people want to do this? There are several reasons. You can make crops more resistant to pests. You can produce fruit and vegetables that are bigger and more regular in shape. In the photo above, scientists are checking apples that have been modified to resist rotting. Some people are against GM foods, however. They say these foods could be unhealthy and that we don't yet know enough about what GM foods can do to people.

Size and Scale

In this book, we measure some things in millimeters and even smaller measurements. This is because inches are just too big for measuring microorganisms and microscopic parts of things. Millimeters are pretty small, and micrometers and **nanometers** are so tiny that they are impossible to see with the naked eye and hard to imagine. There are more than 25 million nanometers in just one inch!

1 inch =	**25.4 millimeters**
1 millimeter =	**1,000 micrometers or 1,000,000 nanometers**
1 micrometer =	**1,000 nanometers**

Only the smallest of microbes are measured in nanometers. Some of these, such as viruses, have to be magnified hundreds of thousands of times before we can see them. Other microorganisms are huge compared to viruses, but we still need to magnify them to see them clearly.

About Microscopes

Many of the images you have looked at were produced using an electron microscope. Electron microscopes can magnify things many thousands of times, so they are used to magnify viruses, bacteria, and tiny parts of cells. They are also used for some of the amazing close-up images of bugs we've seen.

At home or in school, we use optical microscopes. They usually magnify things anywhere between 20 and 1,000 times, depending on the lenses you are using. It's always fun to take an everyday object, like a piece of food or a leaf from the yard, and look at it under the microscope. Some of the images we have seen are made by optical microscopes with cameras attached.

Yeast Balloon

We learned on page 7 that yeast likes to feed on sugar. When it does, it releases carbon dioxide. You can use the gas released by yeast to blow up a balloon.

To do this, you need:

- 1 small balloon
- 1 small plastic soda bottle
- 1 (¼-ounce) packet of active dry yeast
- 1 teaspoon of sugar
- ½ cup of water

1. Stretch the balloon by blowing it up a couple of times and letting it deflate.
2. Warm the water and pour some into the bottle, up to about 1 inch.
3. Add the yeast and swirl it around to mix.
4. Add the sugar and swirl the mixture around some more.
5. Fit the neck of the balloon over the top of the bottle.
6. Leave the bottle standing in a warm place. After a few minutes, you will see the balloon start to inflate. Don't leave it for too long because the balloon might burst.

antibiotic—medicine used to fight infections and illnesses caused by bacteria
bacteria—microorganisms with only one cell that are the smallest and most numerous life-forms on Earth
cell—tiny unit that all livings things are made of
contaminated—infected with harmful organisms or chemicals
cyst—dormant (inactive) stage of a parasite that becomes active when it finds its way into a living host
fermentation—process during which microbes feed on sugars and release products such as alcohol
fungi—organisms similar to plants but with no ability to make food, so they live on other organisms (living or dead).
hyphae—threads that most fungi use to grow and spread through their food source
larva—stage of an insect after it has hatched from an egg but is not yet an adult. *Larvae* is the plural of larva.
microanimal—tiny bug or other animal too small to be seen clearly without a microscope
microbe—microorganism that is not a microanimal. Microbes also include viruses even though they are not really organisms.
microfungi—fungi that are microscopic or are made up mostly of microscopic parts
micrometer—measurement of length that is one-thousandth of a millimeter
microorganism—any living thing that is too small to be seen clearly without a microscope
mites—tiny creatures related to spiders, many of which live on animals, plants, or food
molecule—microscopic part that makes up all living and nonliving things. All cells are made of molecules.
nanometer—measurement of length that is one-millionth of a millimeter
nucleus—part of a cell that controls the cell's form and functions

organism—any living thing, such as a plant, animal, or bacterium
parasite—organism that lives on or in another living thing and feeds off it
protist—usually single-celled microorganism that lives in water or damp places. Protists can be plant-like (algae) or animal-like (protozoa).
species—group of living things of the same kind. For example, bears are a kind of animal, but grizzly bears are a species.
spore—reproductive part of a fungus
starch—form of carbohydrate found in plants
virus—microbe that can only multiply by infecting living cells

Explore These Web Sites

Food Safety & Nutrition Information for Kids and Teens
http://www.fda.gov/food/resourcesforyou/consumers/kidsteens/default.htm
Learn some basic food safety rules.

Genetic Engineering: A Guide for Kids by Tiki the Penguin
http://tiki.oneworld.net/genetics/home.html
Read about DNA, genes, and GM foods.

Microbe Zoo Snack Bar
http://www.commtechlab.msu.edu/sites/dlc-me/zoo/zbmain.html
A Microbe Zoo Web page that looks at microbes in food and drinks.

Molecular Expressions Photo Gallery: Burgers 'n Fries
http://www.micro.magnet.fsu.edu/micro/gallery/burgersnfries/burgersnfries.html
A close-up look at some everyday food.

Index